The Little Volcano Inside

Story by **Ayala Moldawsky**

Illustrated by **Dror Adam**

Contento De Semrik

The Little Volcano Inside
Ayala Moldawsky

Senior editors and producers: Netanel and Osnat Semrik
Translation and Editing: Rechavia Berman
Design: StudioMooza
Illustration: Dror Adam

International sole distributor:
Contento De Semrik
22 Isserles
Tel Aviv 67014, Israel
Semrik10@gmail.com
www.Semrik.com
ISBN: 978-965-7475-55-0

The Little Volcano Inside

Story by **Ayala Moldawsky**

Illustrated by **Dror Adam**

Last night, before I went to bed,
I had the slightest feeling of dread.
And like every time when at night I was bothered,
I went straight to talk with father and mother.
But they were busy, talking so intently
and didn't even notice that I approached and
listened gently.
They said very strange sentences and phrases
and made the most peculiar faces.

I tried to understand what they were saying,
because they even mentioned my name now and
again.
They said "Will is acting out", "disruptive", and
something like "Hyperactive".
Who knows if they meant like Superman or
something really attractive…

I quietly slipped to my cosy room;
I hugged the Teddy I got from Granny Bloom.
But what can I do if my eyes won't close?
The thoughts go 'round and 'round in my head,
playing catch in front and ahead.

Mother said that I interupt
and that I really easily erupt.
And it reminded me how our teacher Natalie
explained once about the eruption of Volcano
Etna in Italy.

I thought to myself about an idea,
and felt that a solution drew near.
Maybe I too have a tiny volcano inside
that erupts whenever something confuses me
deep inside?

Early in the morning, when I got to class,
I played, like always, with my best friend Chas.
He's the only one I told about the "volcano" I
discovered;
Maybe he too has such a volcano, I wondered.

But how can his "volcano" be so quiet?
For Chas doesn't fight and doesn't riot.
When Tomey snatches Chas's ball,
his volcano doesn't erupt and lava doesn't fall!
I asked Chas to tell me the way -
How can he control his volcano all day?
Chas told me that he learned from his father
a way to defeat an opponent without fight or
bother.
Without hitting, cursing, or using violence
with a lot of restraint and a little bit of patience.
If everyone will master the volcano inside,
maybe there won't be any more fights?

And so we've decided, all of us at class,
to form a group and this wisdom to pass.
We added Dean, Jonathan, and Ariel,
and also Bobby, Eddie, and Daniel.
Within about an hour or two,
we got things going after the others joined too.

First we chose a slogan for the group:

**" The one that can master
the volcano within,
Becomes our leader
and so we sing!"**

We told our teacher Natalie too, and with her came
up with a set of rules.
The first rule goes:
Recognize when your mountain is about to erupt,
even though everyone has their own way to know
to recognize when the mountain is about to explode.
Like for instance, before we sneeze,
some folks can tell
by the irritating itch and when
the nose begin to swell.
Or, for example, when we're really hungry,
our stomach makes funny sounds like we have a
monster inside our tummy.

A second important rule:
Try to count to 10
before you lose your cool,
even though just at this crucial minute,
the numbers always get mixed up in it.
And maybe take a breath, deep down,
so that the "volcano" won't be able to turn.
For without oxygen, fire doesn't burn;
breathing helps us calm down and relax
deep down.

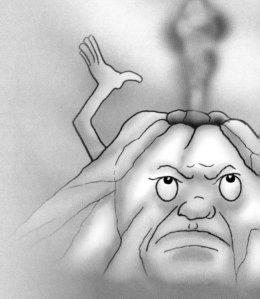

A third and necessary rule:
Instead of immediately lifting your fist,
it's easy, just let go and relax for a bit.
You can walk away,
or think of something to make you feel OK.
For instance, you are brave and strong,
and don't need to hit when treated wrong.

A fourth rule should definitely be:
That not everything is all about me.
If Adam dropped our crayons on the floor,
it could be an accident and nothing more.
We can say "Please be careful",and that's all.!
And if Ashley didn't invite me to her birthday,
maybe she just forgot and still wants to play.

And if nothing works out,
and the volcano tries hard to spout,
we can try to drink a glass of water or two.
Maybe that can make the "volcano" subdue.

      When I get this,
      then, in myself I can believe,
      and the "volcano" can remain asleep,
      stay quiet, and won't make a peep.

At the end of the day,
our teacher Natalie told us happily:
"Our exercise passed very successfully.
I think that, finally, there are no active volcanoes
left in our class".

And so at night, before I fell asleep,
I had the most joyful release.
I went straight to Mom and Dad
and told them about the volcano I had,
and how it can be controlled
without much trouble at all.
They were so proud, Mom and Dad,
and decided to adopt the rules that I made.
I think that tonight I'll dream of places so
awesome and glad…

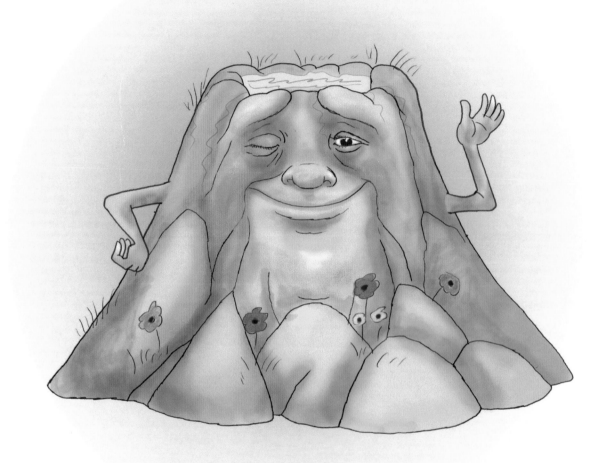

And what about you? What makes your volcano erupt?
Or that only happens to the friend by your side…